Boublil & Schönberg's
Do You Hear the People Sing

ISBN 978-1-4584-1556-1

HAL•LEONARD®
CORPORATION

7777 W. BLUEMOUND RD. P.O. BOX 13819 MILWAUKEE, WI 53213

Visit Hal Leonard Online at
www.halleonard.com

Do You Hear the People Sing – The Dream Concert

Over 30 years ago, the creative team of Alain Boublil and Claude-Michel Schönberg changed the history of musical theatre with their masterpiece, *Les Misérables*. *Do You Hear the People Sing* celebrates music of two of the world's most prolific writers of musical theatre in one unforgettable concert with music from *Les Misérables, Miss Saigon* and much more, plus moments never before heard and many surprises. This extraordinary new concert is brought to you by BOUBERG PRODUCTIONS and IMG artists.

Maureen Taylor
Orchestral Pops
Booking Manager
mtaylor@imgartists.com
212.994.3535

Dramatic Performance Rights for *Les Misérables*, *Miss Saigon* and *Martin Guerre*
controlled and licensed by
Cameron Mackintosh (Overseas) Ltd.
One Bedford Square, London WC1B 3RA England
Tel (171) 637-8866 Fax (171) 436-2683

Dramatic Performance Rights for *Pirate Queen*
controlled and licensed by
Bouberg Productions
c/o Joel Faden & Co., Inc., MLM 250 West 57th St., 26th Floor, New York, NY 10107
Tel. (212) 246-7203, Fax (212) 246-7217, mwlock@joelfaden.com

Dramatic Performance Rights for *La Revolution Française*
controlled and licensed by
Alain Boublil Music Ltd.
c/o Joel Faden & Co., Inc., MLM 250 West 57th St., 26th Floor, New York, NY 10107
Tel. (212) 246-7203, Fax (212) 246-7217, mwlock@joelfaden.com

Stock and Amateur Performance Rights are licensed by
Music Theater International, Inc.
421 West 54th St., New York, NY 10019
Tel (212) 541-4684 Fax (212) 397-4684
Licensing@MTIshows.com

Non-Dramatic and Concert Performance Rights are controlled by
Alain Boublil Music Ltd. (ASCAP)
c/o Joel Faden & Co., Inc., MLM 250 West 57th St., 26th Floor, New York, NY 10107
Tel. (212) 246-7203, Fax (212) 246-7217, mwlock@joelfaden.com

BUI-DOI

from MISS SAIGON

Music by CLAUDE-MICHEL SCHÖNBERG
Lyrics by RICHARD MALTBY, JR. and ALAIN BOUBLIL
Adapted from original French Lyrics by ALAIN BOUBLIL

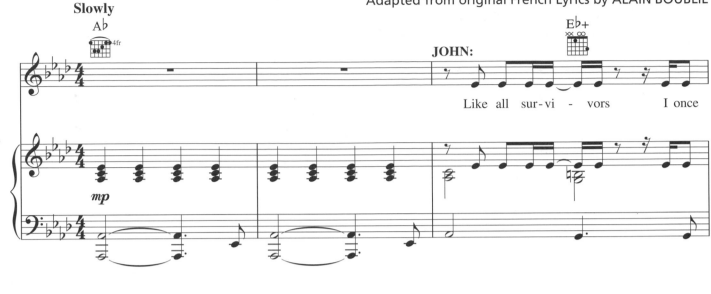

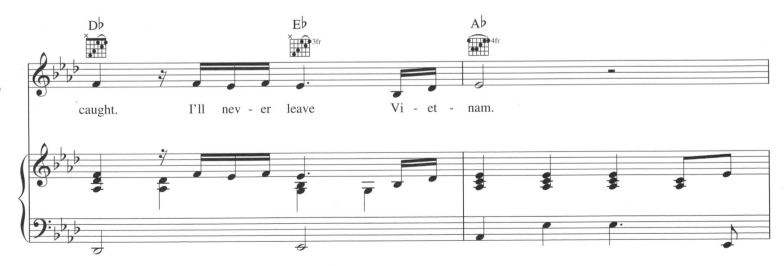

War is-n't o-ver _____ when it ends. _____ Some pic-tures nev-er leave _ your mind.

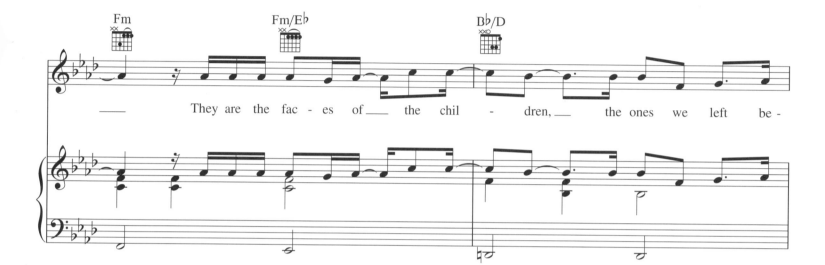

_____ They are the fac-es of _____ the chil-dren, _____ the ones we left be-

hind. _____ They're called Bui-doi, _____ the dust of life, _____ con-ceived in

hell _____ and born in strife. They are the liv-ing re-min-der of

all the good we failed to do. That's why we know, deep in our hearts, that they are

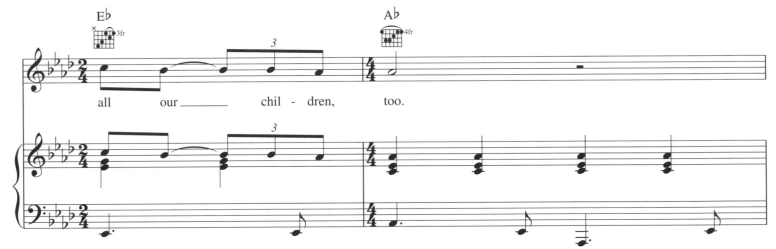

all our _____ chil - dren, too.

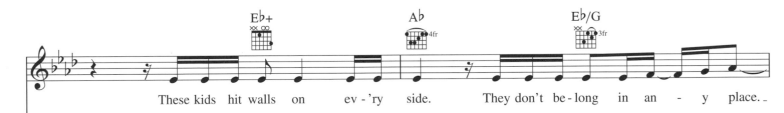

These kids hit walls on ev-'ry side. They don't be-long in an - y place.

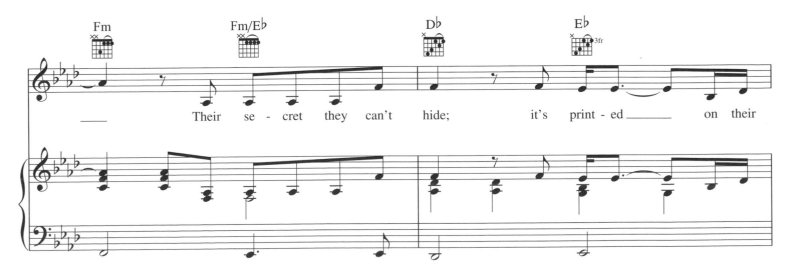

_____ Their se - cret they can't hide; it's print - ed _____ on their

face. I nev-er thought one day I'd plead

for half-breeds from a land that's torn. But then I saw a camp for chil-

-dren whose crime was be-ing born. They're called Bui-

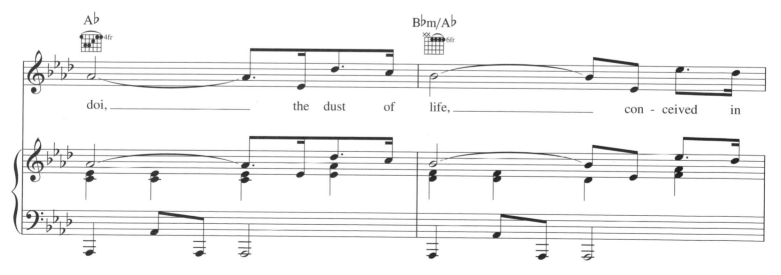

doi, the dust of life, con-ceived in

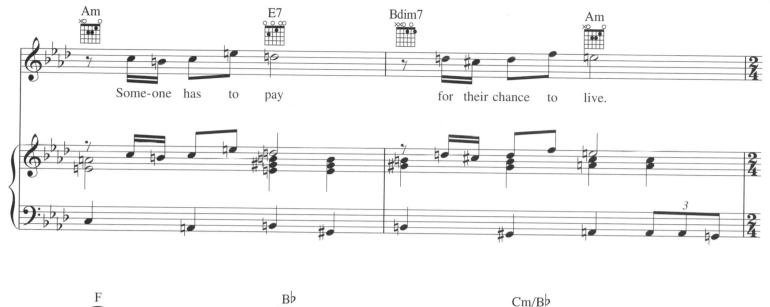

Some-one has to pay for their chance to live.

JOHN: Help me try.

MEN: They're called Bui - doi, the dust of life, con-ceived in

hell and born in strife. They are the liv - ing re - min - der of

They are the liv - ing re - min - der of

THE HEAT IS ON IN SAIGON

from MISS SAIGON

Music by CLAUDE-MICHEL SCHÖNBERG
Lyrics by RICHARD MALTBY, Jr. and ALAIN BOUBLIL
Adapted from Original French Lyrics by ALAIN BOUBLIL

Driving beat

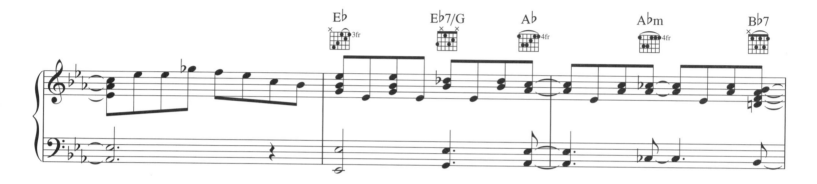

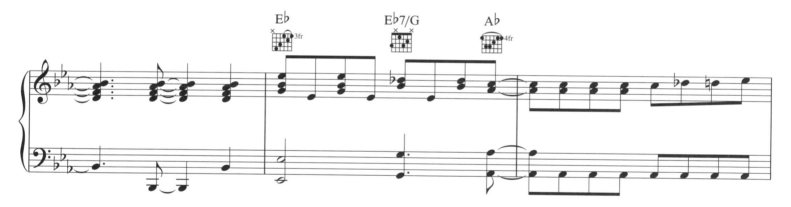

AMERICANS:

The heat is on in Sai-gon. ___ The girls are hot-ter 'n hell. _

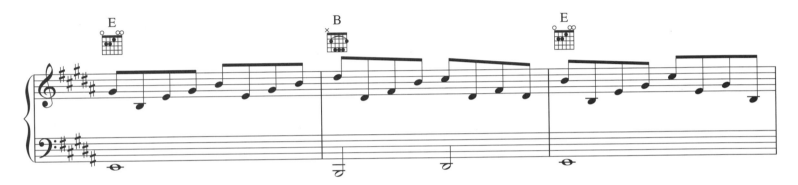

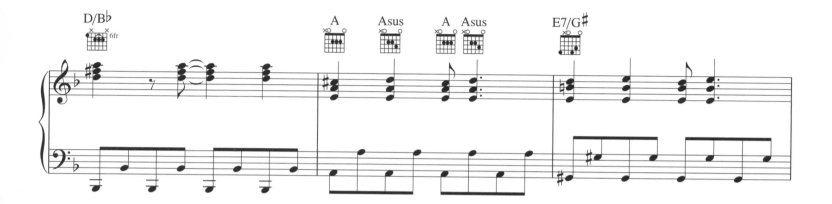

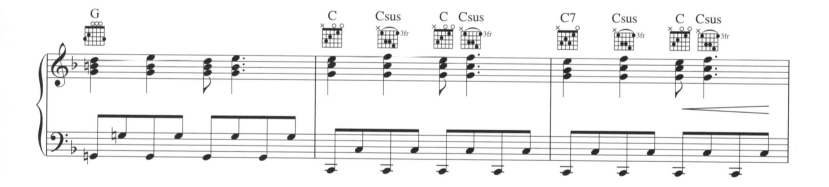

The heat is on in Sai- gon.

And things are not go- ing well.

But still at mid-night the par-ty goes on, ___

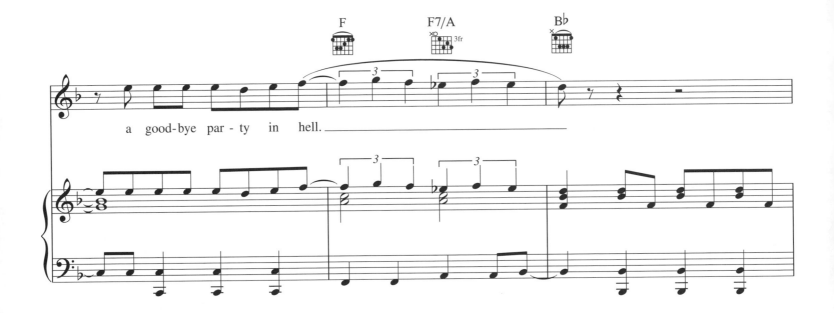

a good-bye par-ty in hell. ___

I'D GIVE MY LIFE FOR YOU

from MISS SAIGON

Music by CLAUDE-MICHEL SCHÖNBERG
Lyrics by RICHARD MALTBY, JR. and ALAIN BOUBLIL
Adapted from original French Lyrics by ALAIN BOUBLIL

Slowly, with expression

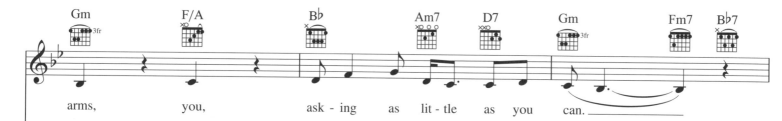

20

brought you here. ___ And in one per-fect night when the stars burned like

new, I knew what I must do. I'll

give you ___ a mil-lion things I'll nev-er own, I'll give you ___ a world to con-quer when you're

grown. You will be who you want to be. ___ You

grants. _____ As long as you can have your chance,

I swear I'll give my life for you. No one can stop what I must

do. I swear I'll give my life for you.

THE LAST NIGHT OF THE WORLD
from MISS SAIGON

Music by CLAUDE-MICHEL SCHÖNBERG
Lyrics by RICHARD MALTBY, JR. and ALAIN BOUBLIL
Adapted from original French Lyrics by ALAIN BOUBLIL

Languidly

CHRIS: In a place that won't let us feel, ___

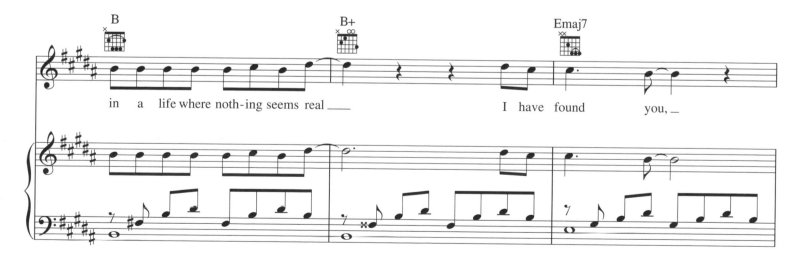

in a life where noth-ing seems real ___ I have found you, ___

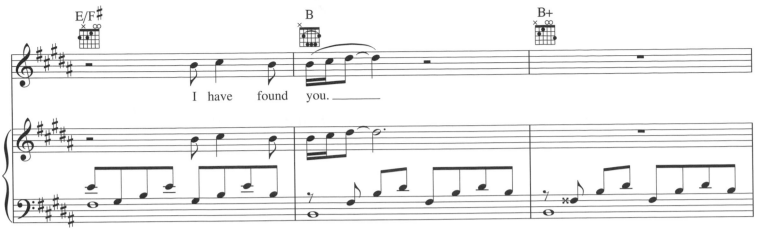

I have found you. _____

KIM:
In a world that's mov-ing too fast, ___ in a world where noth-ing can last, ___

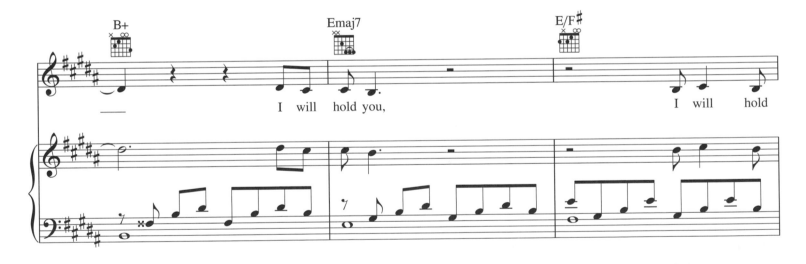

___ I will hold you, I will hold

you. ___ CHRIS: Our lives will change when to-mor-row comes. ___ KIM: To-night our

hearts dream the dis - tant drums. _____ And we have

mu - sic al - right __ tear - ing the night. _ A song

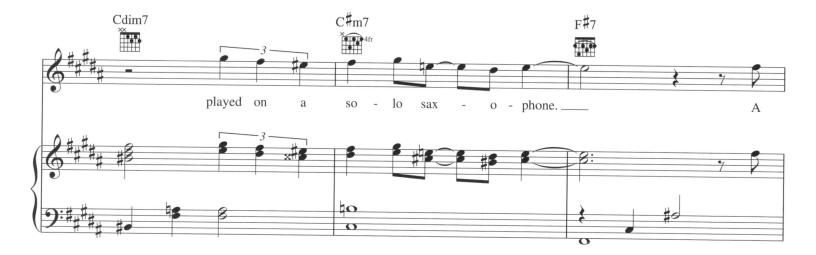

played on a so - lo sax - o - phone. _____

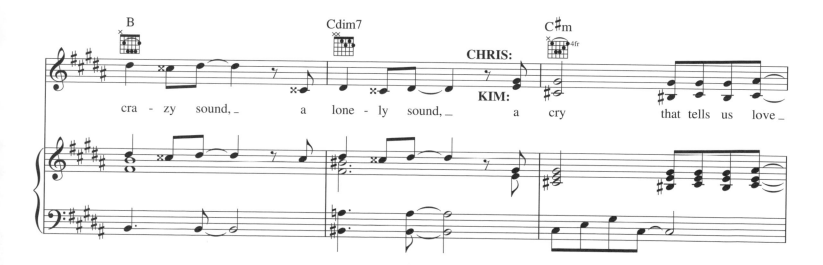

cra - zy sound, _ a lone - ly sound, _ a cry that tells us love _

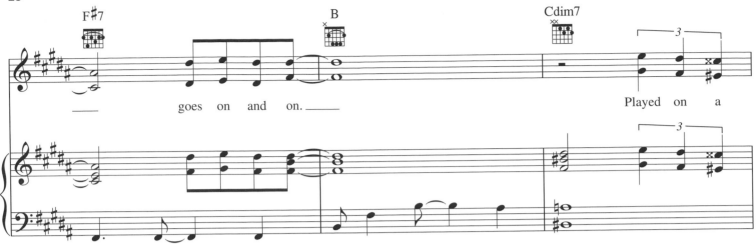

goes on and on. _____ Played on a

so - lo sax - o - phone, _____ it's tell - ing me _____ to

hold you tight _____ and dance like it's the last _____ night of the

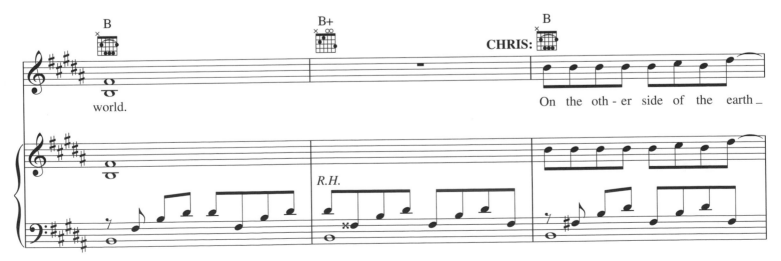

world. B+ **CHRIS:** B

On the oth - er side of the earth _

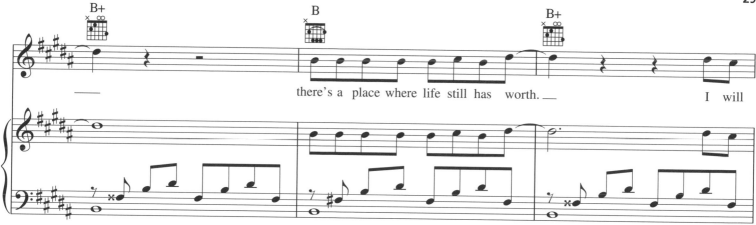

there's a place where life still has worth.____ I will

take you.

KIM: I'll go with you.____ **CHRIS:** You won't be-

lieve all the things you'll see.____ I know 'cause you'll see them all with me.__

CHRIS:
KIM:
If we're to - geth - er, well then, we'll hear it a - gain, a

song played on a so - lo sax - o - phone, __

__ A cra - zy sound, __ a lone - ly sound, __ a

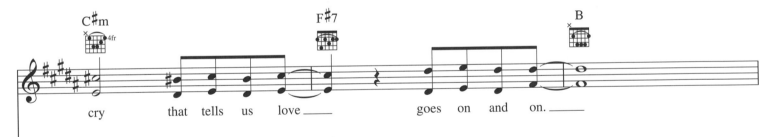

cry that tells us love __ goes on and on. __

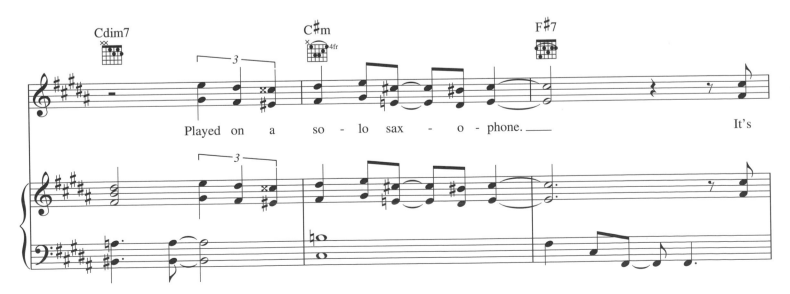

Played on a so - lo sax - o - phone. __ It's

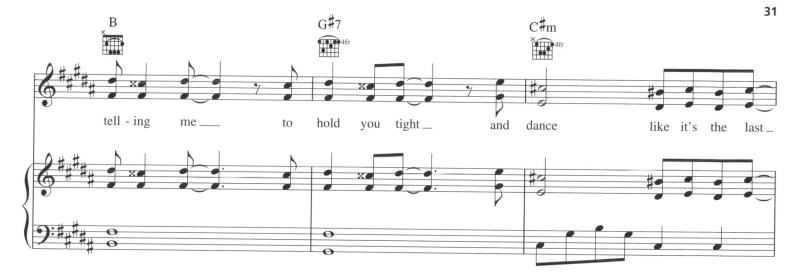

tell - ing me ___ to hold you tight ___ and dance like it's the last ___

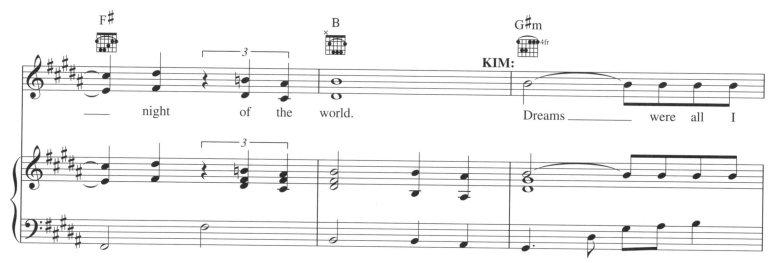

___ night of the world.

KIM: Dreams ___ were all I

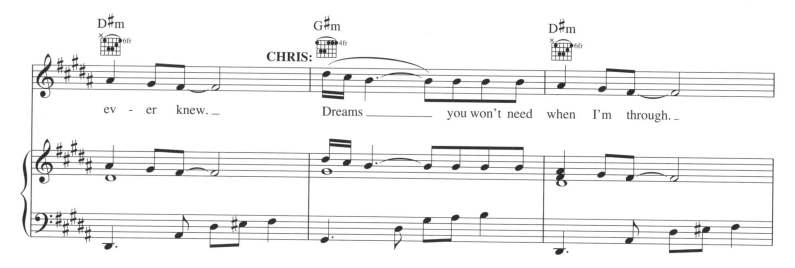

ev - er knew. ___

CHRIS: Dreams ___ you won't need when I'm through. ___

BOTH: An - y - where we may be

CHRIS: I will sing ___ with

KIM:

Maestoso

you our song.

CHRIS:

KIM: So stay with me _____ and

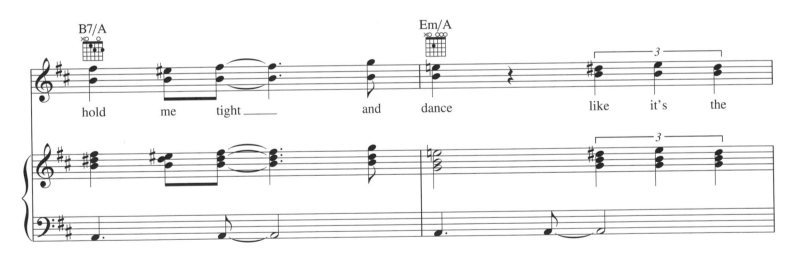

hold me tight _____ and dance like it's the

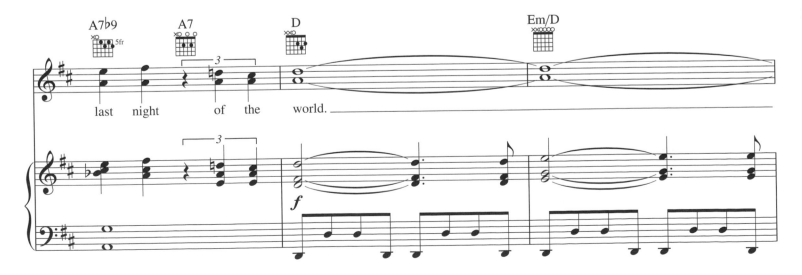

last night of the world. _____

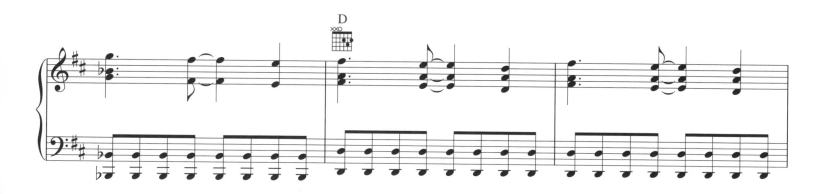

NOW THAT I'VE SEEN HER

from MISS SAIGON

Music by CLAUDE-MICHEL SCHÖNBERG
Lyrics by RICHARD MALTBY, JR. and ALAIN BOUBLIL
Adapted from original French Lyrics by ALAIN BOUBLIL

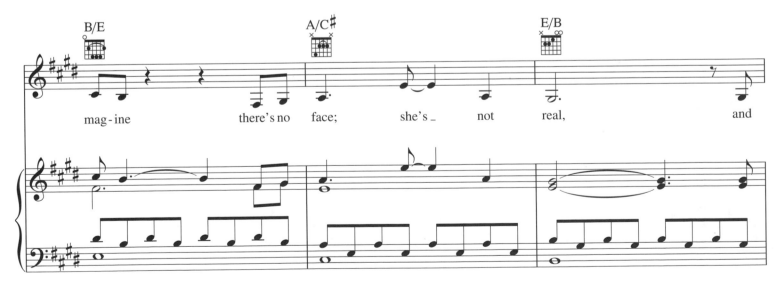

you can tell your-self it's all O - K. But she's here

and my heart cries this is - n't

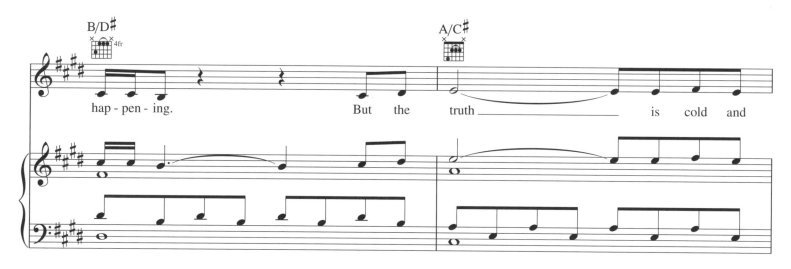

hap - pen - ing. But the truth _____ is cold and

real, _____ and I know this storm _____ won't go a - way.

Now that ___ I've seen her, ___ there's no way ___ to

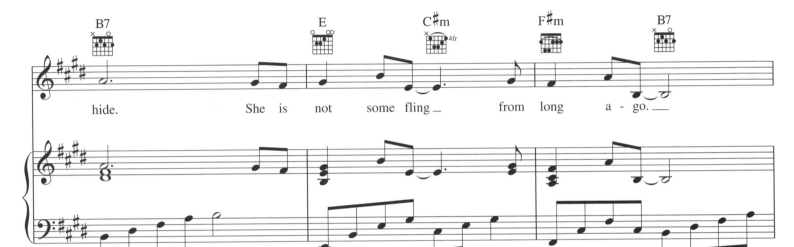

hide. She is not some fling ___ from long a - go. ___

Now that ___ I've seen her, ___ I know why ___ he

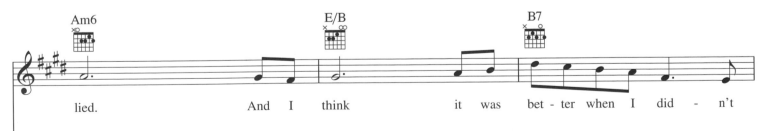

lied. And I think it was bet - ter when I did - n't

know. _____

In her eyes, _____ in her

rit. *a tempo*

voice, _____ in the heat _____ that filled the

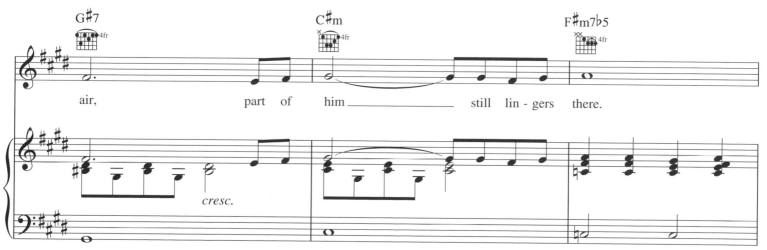

air, _____ part of him _____ still lin - gers there.

cresc.

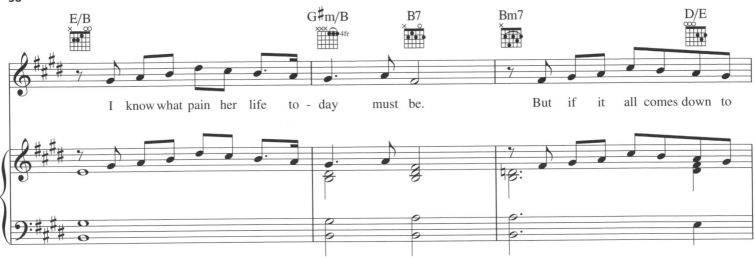

I know what pain her life to-day must be. But if it all comes down to

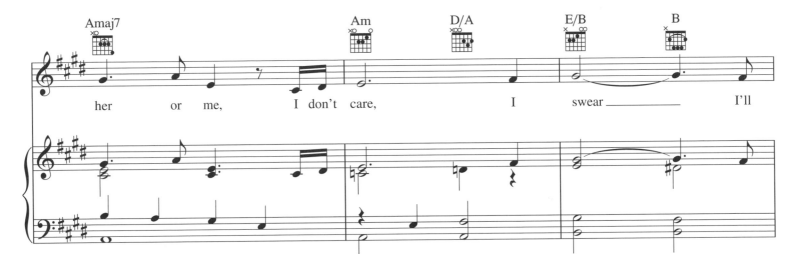

her or me, I don't care, I swear _____ I'll

fight.

Now that ___ I've seen her, ___ she's more than ___ a

name.   I don't hate this girl, __ e - ven so. __

Now that __ I've seen her, __ I can't stay __ the

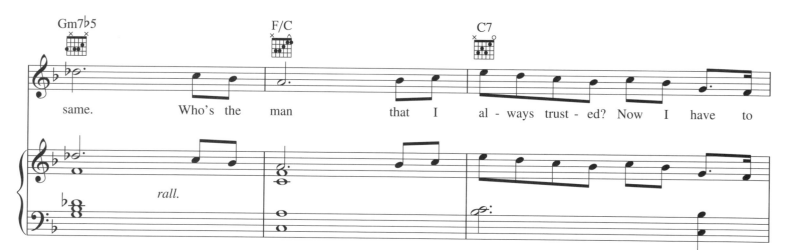

same.   Who's the man   that I al - ways trust - ed? Now I have to

rall.

know. _____

f a tempo

THE AMERICAN DREAM
from MISS SAIGON

Music by CLAUDE-MICHEL SCHÖNBERG
Lyrics by RICHARD MALTBY, JR. and ALAIN BOUBLIL
Adapted from original French Lyrics by ALAIN BOUBLIL

they're my fam - 'ly. They're sell - ing what peo - ple need.

What's that I smell in the air, ___ the A - mer - i - can dream. _

Sweet as a new mil - lion - aire, ___ the A - mer - i - can dream. _

___ Pre - packed and read - y to wear, _

the A-mer-i-can dream.

Fat, like a choc-'late e-clair, ___ when you suck out the cream. ___

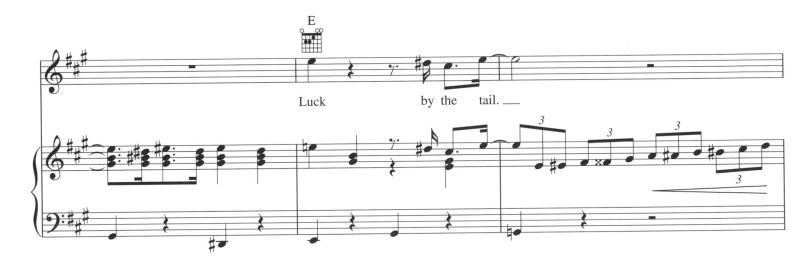

Luck ___ by the tail. ___

How ___ can you fail? ___ And best of all, it's for sale, ___

the A-mer-i-can dream.

Lightly

Greas-y chinks _ make life so sleaz - y. _ In the states _ I'll build a

club that's four - starred. _ Men like me _ there have things eas - y. _

They have a law-yer and a bod-y - guard. _ To the johns there _

the A-mer - i-can dream.

Bald peo - ple think they'll grow hair, ___ the A-mer - i-can dream. _

Call girls are lin - ing Times Square, _ the A-mer - i-can dream. _

Girls can buy tits by the pair, _

the A-mer-i-can dream. ___

Bald peo-ple think they'll grow hair, ___ the A-mer-i-can dream. ___

On stage each night Fred As-taire, ___ the A-mer-i-can dream. ___

___ Schlitz down the drain. ___

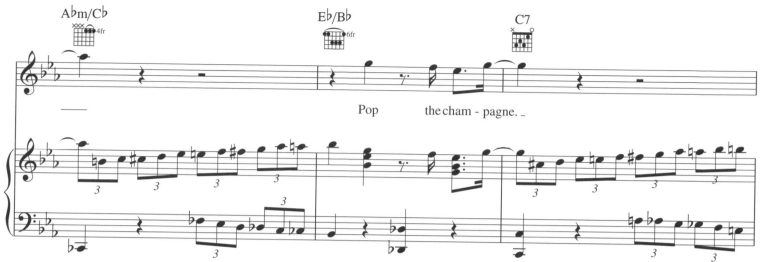

Pop the cham - pagne. _

It's time we all en - ter - tain ___ my A - mer - i - can dream. _

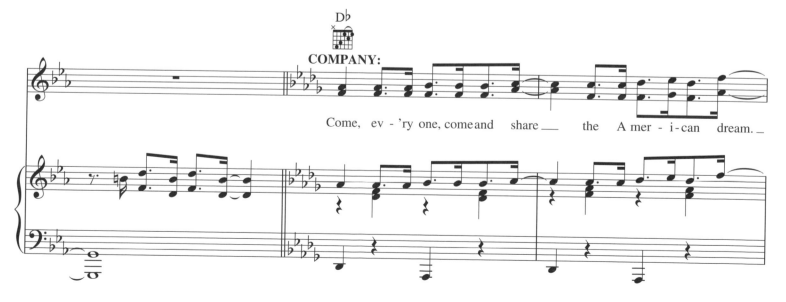

COMPANY:

Come, ev - 'ry one, come and share ___ the A - mer - i - can dream. _

Name what you want and it's there, ___

___ the A-mer-i-can dream. ___

Spend and have mon-ey to spare, ___ the A-mer-i-can dream. ___

Live like you have-n't a care ___ the A-mer-i-can dream. ___

ENGINEER:

There   I will crown _

Miss Chi - na - town. _

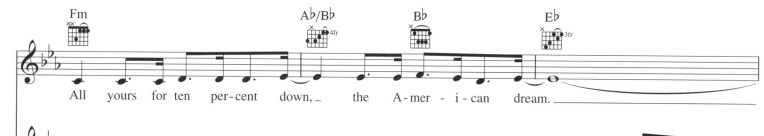

All   yours for ten   per-cent down, _ the A-mer - i - can dream. _

I'M MARTIN GUERRE

from MARTIN GUERRE

Music by CLAUDE-MICHEL SCHÖNBERG
Lyrics by ALAIN BOUBLIL and STEPHEN CLARK

all a young man needs is time. Damn them all!

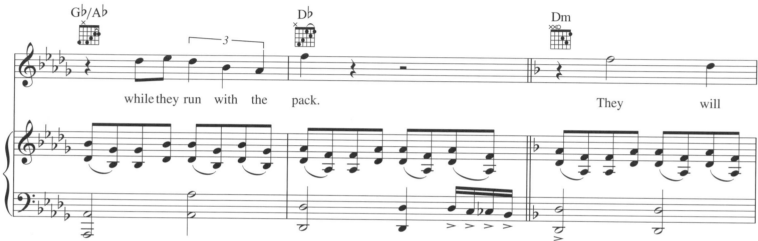

while they run with the pack. They will

pay for the scars on my back.

Look...   *Look...*

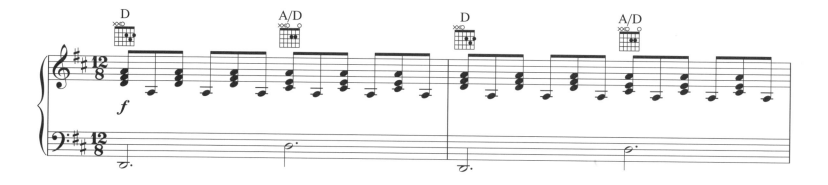

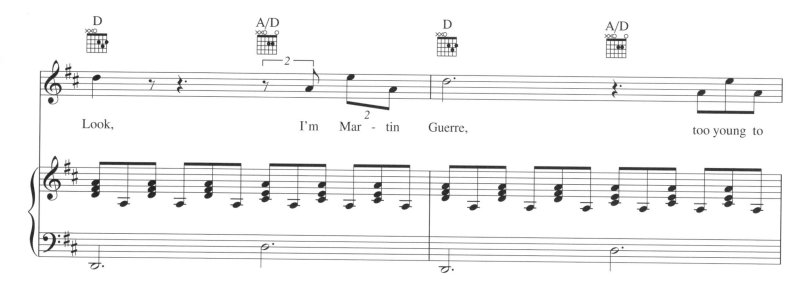

Look,   I'm Mar - tin   Guerre,   too young to

love,   but still a - bove   the lie they   live.

Then I trust-ed the priest, now my blood runs like wine. And then there was Ber - trande. It seems all love must turn to

dust, there must be some - one I can trust.

rit.

Poco meno mosso che prima

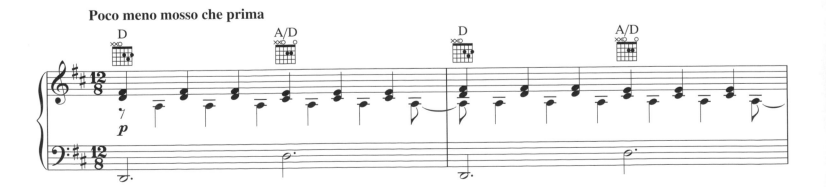

Soon _____ you __ will see _____ that

I can choose to __ be free. They

all look for some-one to blame but I swear it a-

loud, I ___ will be proud I'm __ Mar-tin Guerre. They

all look for some - one to blame, but I swear it a -

loud, I ___ will be proud that __ Mar - tin Guerre _____ is my

Dm

name! _____

ff

ff

LIVE WITH SOMEBODY YOU LOVE

from MARTIN GUERRE

Music by CLAUDE-MICHEL SCHÖNBERG
Lyrics by ALAIN BOUBLIL and STEPHEN CLARK

For solo version: soloist should sing top line and make bars marked ✱ instrumental.

64

I DREAMED A DREAM
from LES MISÉRABLES

Music by CLAUDE-MICHEL SCHÖNBERG
Lyrics by ALAIN BOUBLIL, JEAN-MARC NATEL
and HERBERT KRETZMER

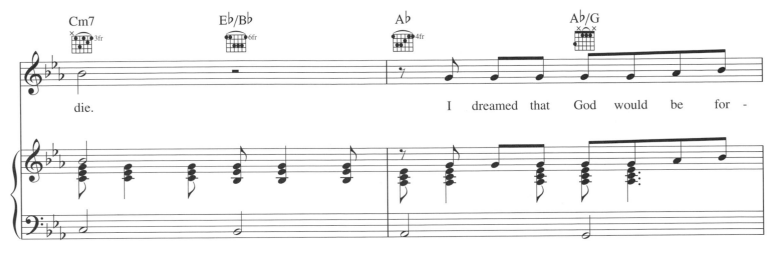

die. I dreamed that God would be for -

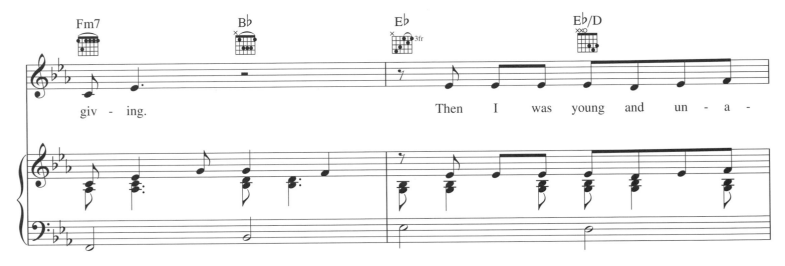

giv - ing. Then I was young and un - a -

fraid, and dreams were made and used and

wast - ed. _____ There was no ran - som to be

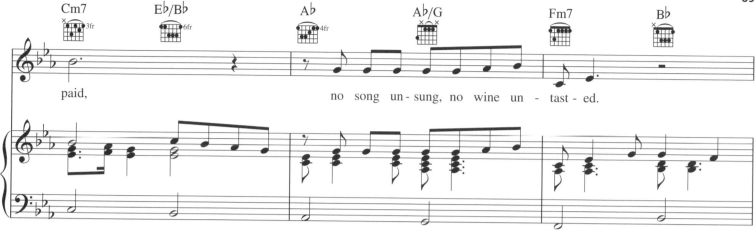

paid, no song un-sung, no wine un - tast - ed.

poco più mosso

But the ti - gers come at night with their voic - es soft as

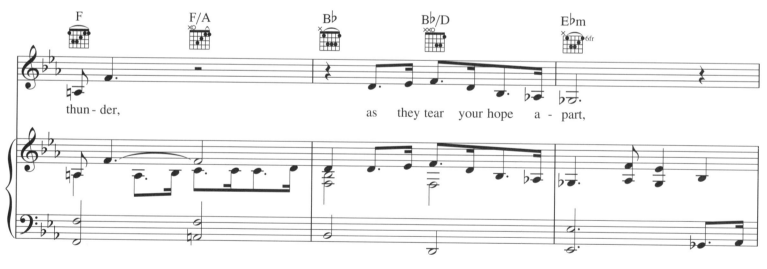

thun - der, as they tear your hope a - part,

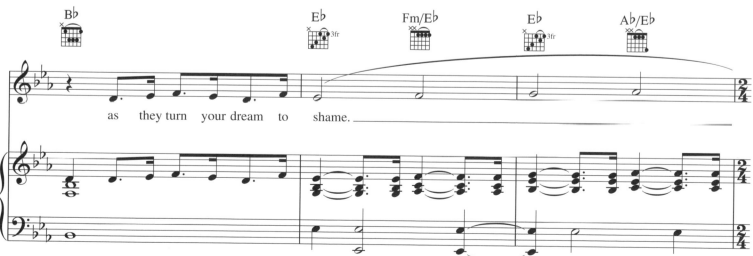

as they turn your dream to shame.

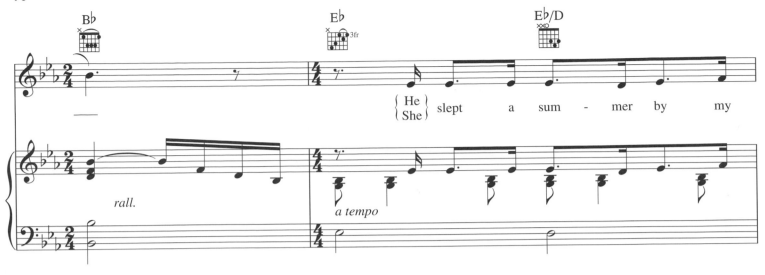

{He / She} slept a sum - mer by my

side.

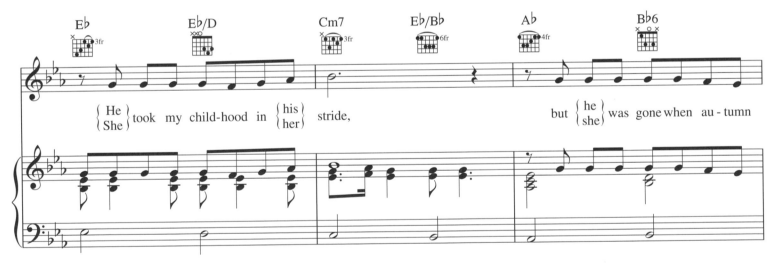

{He / She} filled my days with end - less won - der.

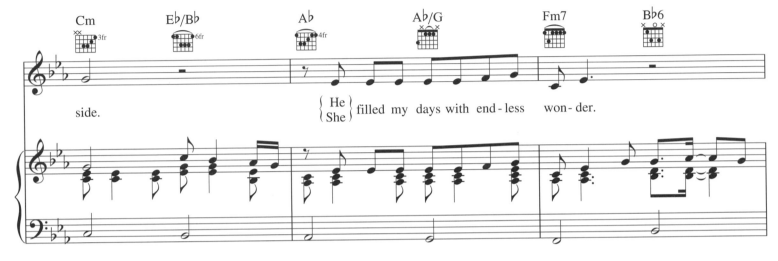

{He / She} took my child-hood in {his / her} stride, but {he / she} was gone when au - tumn

came.

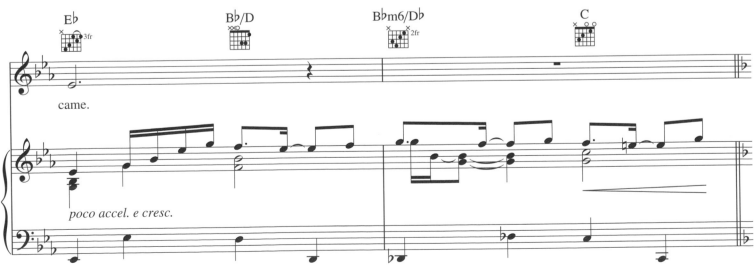

poco accel. e cresc.

be so dif-f'rent from this hell I'm

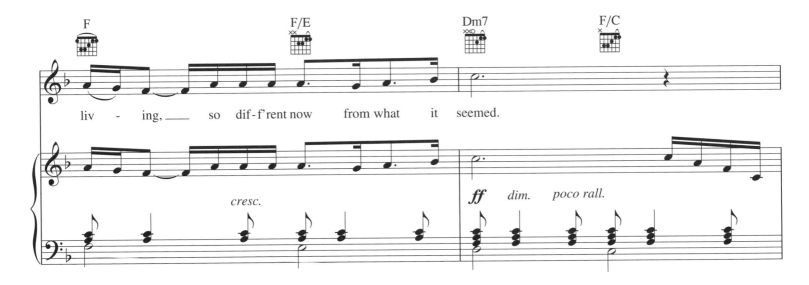

liv - ing,___ so dif-f'rent now from what it seemed.

cresc. *ff dim. poco rall.*

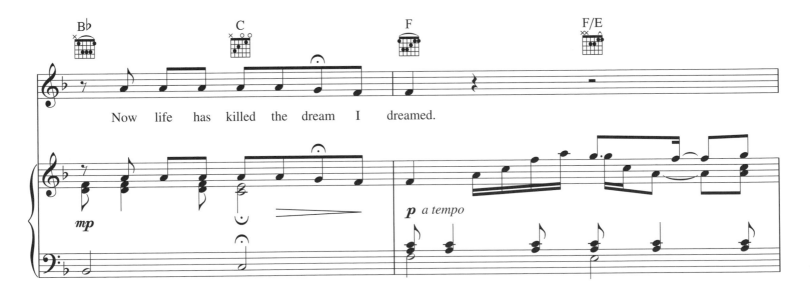

Now life has killed the dream I dreamed.

mp *p a tempo*

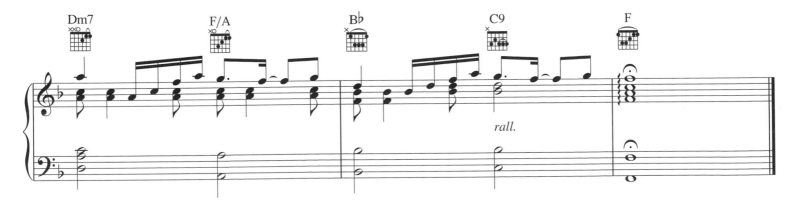

rall.

WOMAN
from THE PIRATE QUEEN

Music by CLAUDE-MICHEL SCHÖNBERG
Lyrics by ALAIN BOUBLIL, RICHARD MALTBY, JR.
and JOHN DEMPSEY

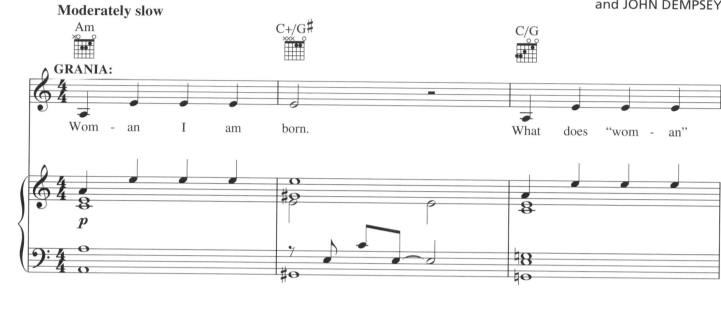

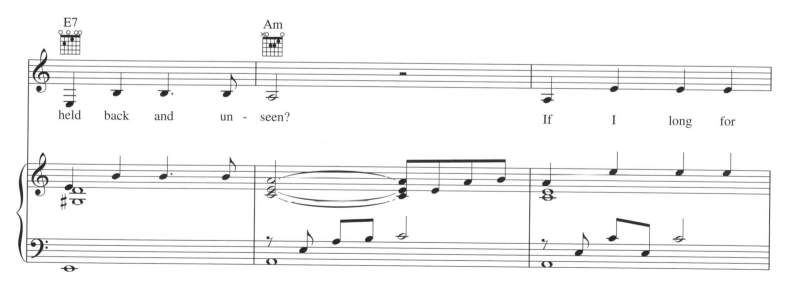

fire, must it stay un - real?

Can I not de - sire? Am I not to

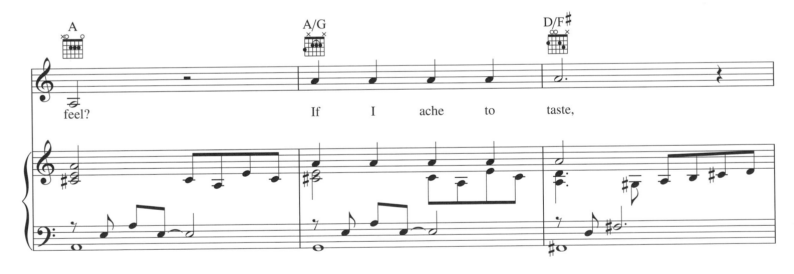

feel? If I ache to taste,

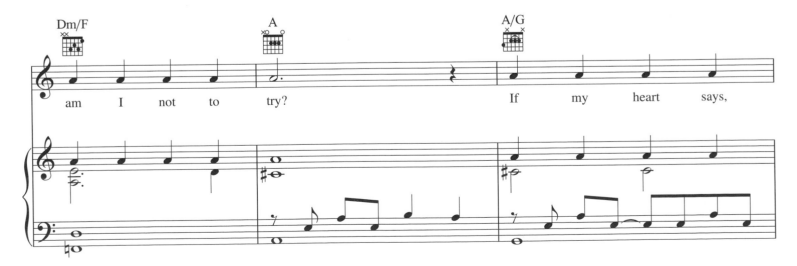

am I not to try? If my heart says,

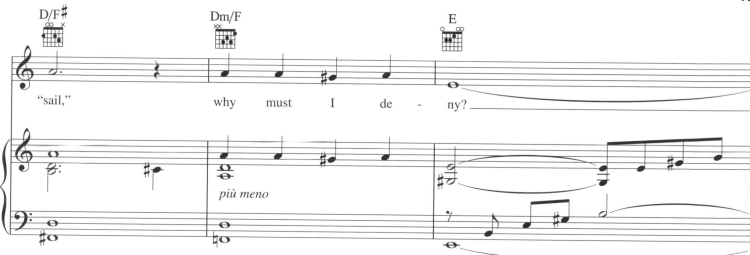

"sail," why must I de - ny? _____

più meno

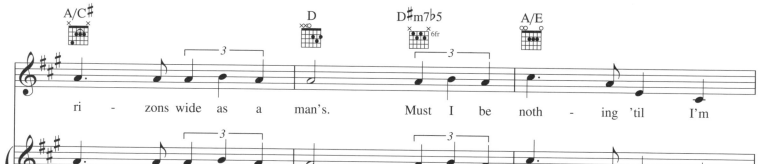

In 2

— I have my dreams, I have made plans. I see ho -

mp *a tempo*

ri - zons wide as a man's. Must I be noth - ing 'til I'm

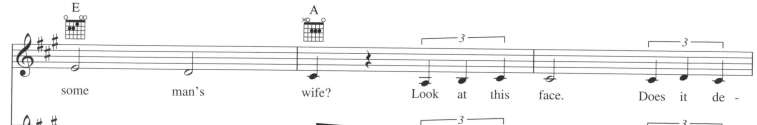

some man's wife? Look at this face. Does it de -

ceive? Do I look made to milk and to weave? I will be

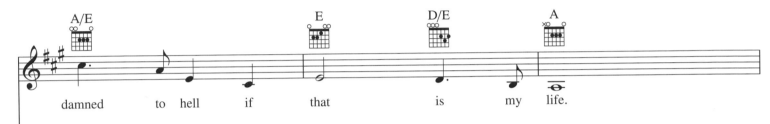

damned to hell if that is my life.

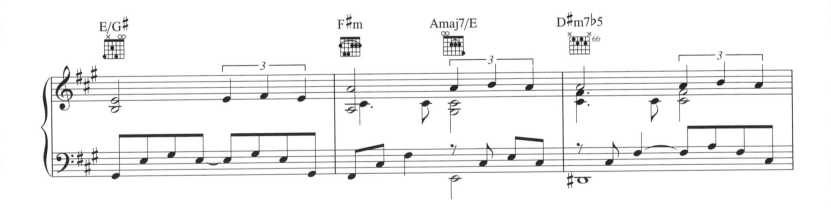

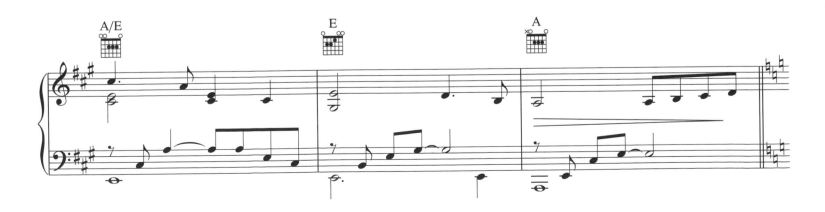

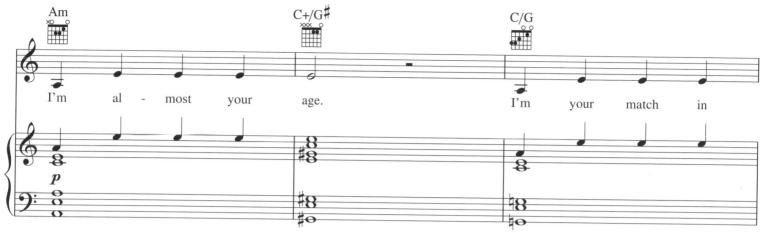

I'm al - most your age.   I'm your match in

size.   I'm your match with swords,   an

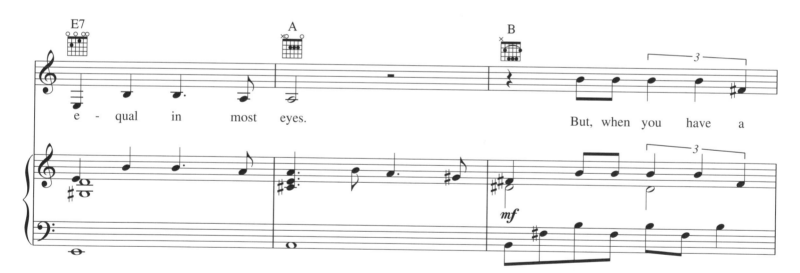

e - qual in most eyes.   But, when you have a

dream   and you're caught in its grip,

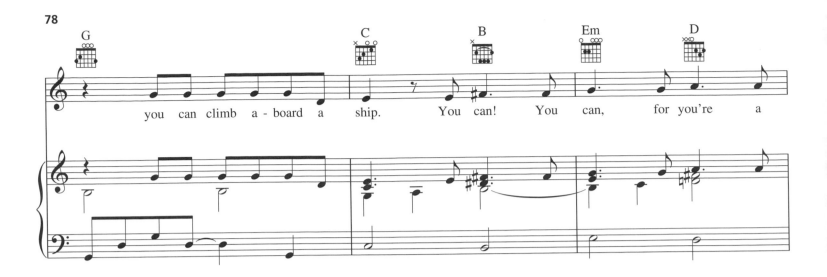

you can climb a-board a ship. You can! You can, for you're a

man. You can reach t'ward that place where the earth meets the sky,

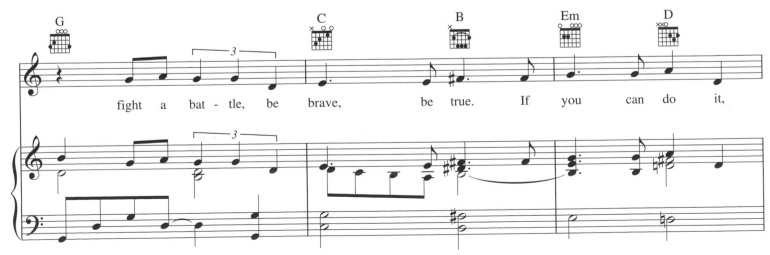

fight a bat-tle, be brave, be true. If you can do it,

IF I SAID I LOVED YOU

from THE PIRATE QUEEN

Music by CLAUDE-MICHEL SCHÖNBERG
Lyrics by ALAIN BOUBLIL, RICHARD MALTBY, JR.
and JOHN DEMPSEY

TIERNAN:
If I said I loved you,
all my life I loved you,
would the line be crossed? Would the words make sense?

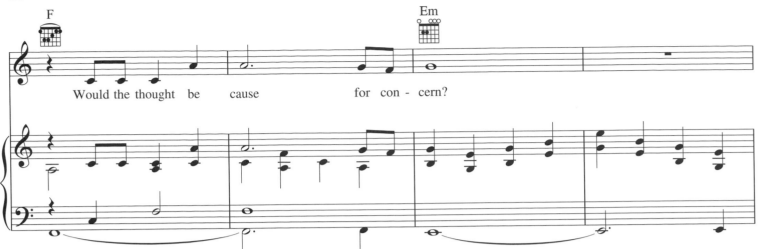

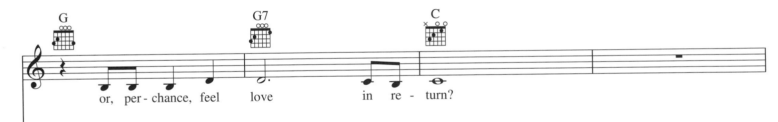

loved you, would you think me cruel

to pre-sume as much? Should I take more time to de-

clare? Would I seem the fool

to ad-mit as such? In my heart, you've al - ways been

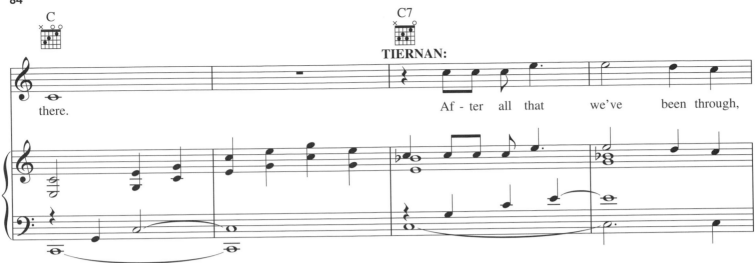

TIERNAN:

After all that we've been through,
there.

GRANIA:

is it now too late? Is it too soon?

Can a man for - give? Were the wounds you bore giv - en
time to heal?

TIERNAN:

Af - ter so much time can the

seed still grow? _____ Can there still be fire in this

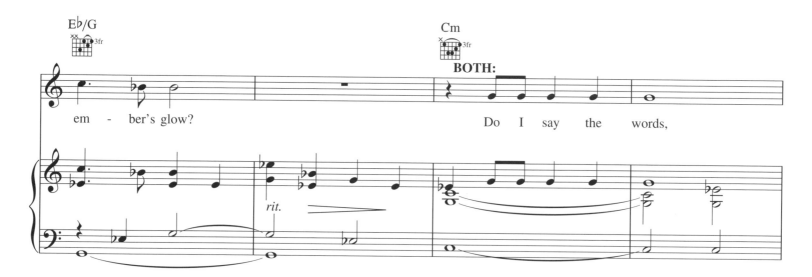

em - ber's glow? **BOTH:** Do I say the words,

risk as few would dare such a pre-cious bond as we

share?

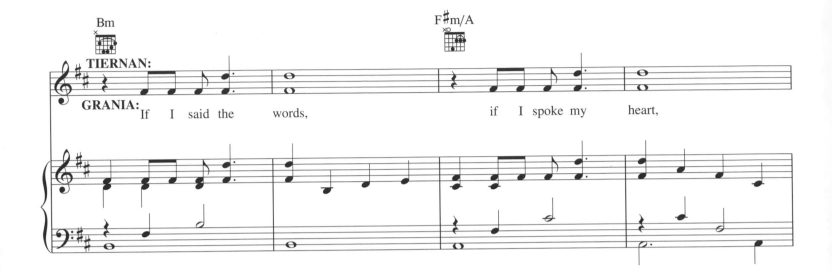

TIERNAN:

GRANIA: If I said the words, if I spoke my heart,

if I said out loud what I feel, _____

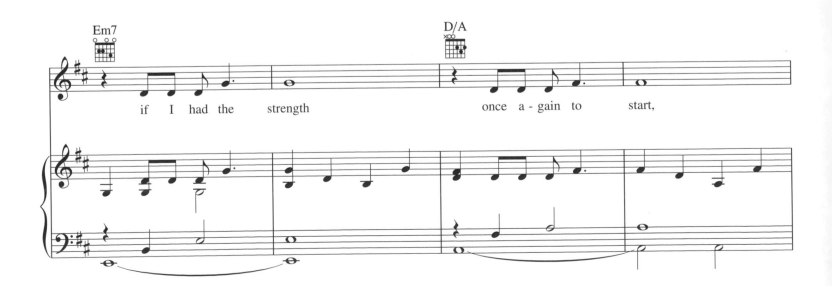

if I had the strength once a - gain to start,

I would risk the tide and re-veal it all. I

wonder what you'd say, wonder what you'd do,

if I said, my love, "I love you."

ON MY OWN
from LES MISÉRABLES

Music by CLAUDE-MICHEL SCHÖNBERG
Lyrics by ALAIN BOUBLIL, JEAN-MARC NATEL,
HERBERT KRETZMER, JOHN CAIRD
and TREVOR NUNN

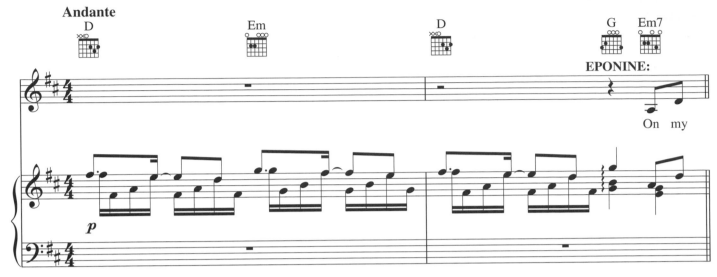

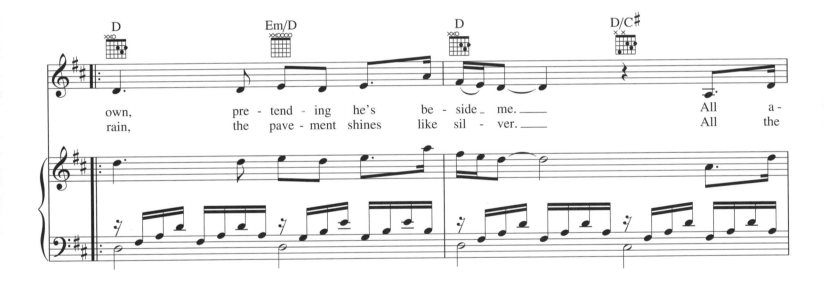

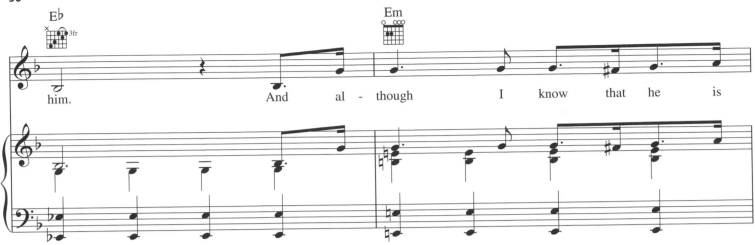

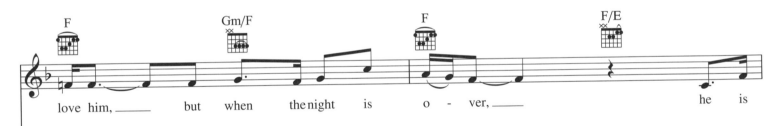

out him the world a-round me chang - es. The

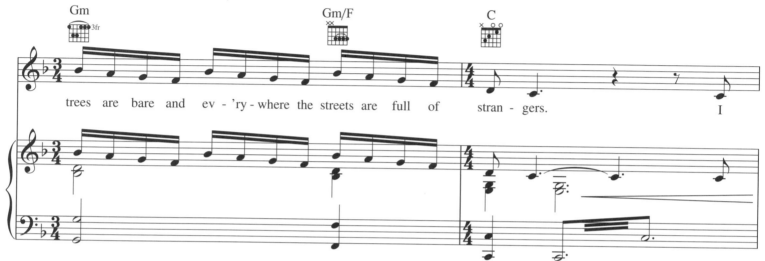

trees are bare and ev-'ry-where the streets are full of stran - gers. I

love him_____ but ev-'ry day I'm learn - ing_____ all my

life I've on - ly been pre-tend - ing._____ With -

out me his world will go on turn - ing. _____ The

world is full of hap - pi - ness that I have nev - er known.

I

love him, _____

I love him, _____

I

love him, _____ but on - ly on my own.

rall.

AT THE END OF THE DAY
from LES MISÉRABLES

Music by CLAUDE-MICHEL SCHÖNBERG
Lyrics by ALAIN BOUBLIL, JEAN-MARC NATEL
and HERBERT KRETZMER

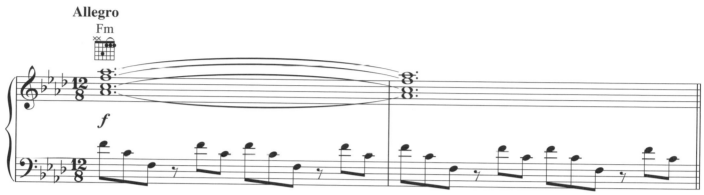

THE POOR:

At the end of the day you're an-oth-er day old-er.
At the end of the day you're an-oth-er day cold-er.

And that's all you can say for the life of the poor.
And the shirt on your back does-n't keep out the chill.

It's a
And the

struggle, __ it's a war.
right - eous __ hur - ry past.

And there's noth - ing that an - y - one's giv - ing. One more
They don't hear the lit - tle ones cry - ing. And the

day stand - ing a - bout, what is it for?
win - ter is com - ing on fast, read - y to kill.

1

One less day to be liv - ing.
One day near - er to

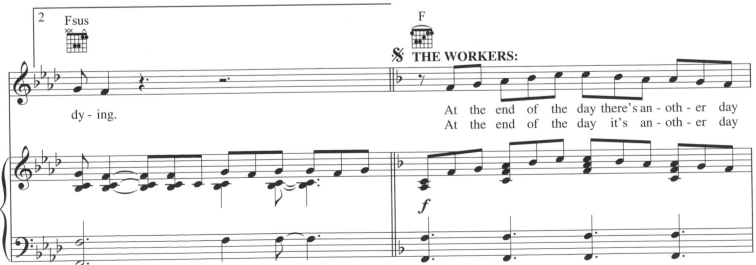

2 Fsus

dy - ing.

𝄋 **THE WORKERS:**

At the end of the day there's an - oth - er day
At the end of the day it's an - oth - er day

dawn- ing.
o - ver,

And the sun in the morn- ing is wait- ing to
with e - nough in your pock - et to last for a

rise.
week.

Like the waves crash_ on the sand,
Pay the land - lord, _ pay the shop.

like a
Keep on

storm that -'ll break an - y sec - ond, there's a hun - ger _ in the land.
graft - ing as long as you're a - ble. Keep on graft - ing _ till you drop,

There's a
or it's

reck - on - ing still to be reck - oned. And there's gon - na be hell _ to
back to the crumbs off the ta - ble. Well, you've got to pay _ your

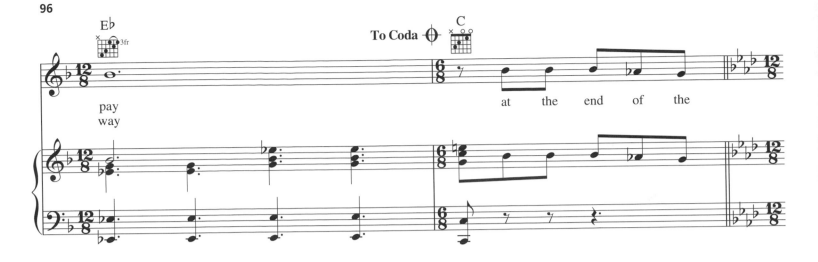

pay
way

at the end of the

day.

FOREMAN:

At the end of the day you get noth-ing for

noth-ing.

Sit-ting flat on your butt does-n't buy an-y

bread.

WORKER 1:

There are chil-dren___ back at home.

WORKERS 1 & 2:

And the

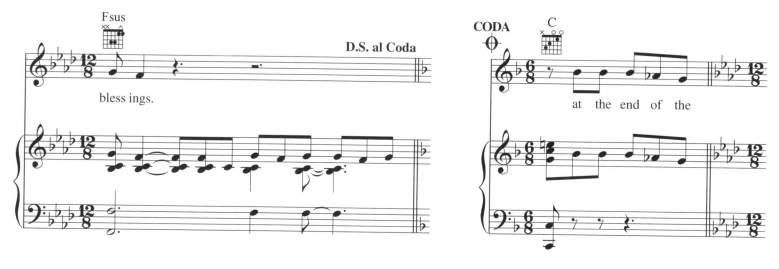

MASTER OF THE HOUSE

from LES MISÉRABLES

Music by CLAUDE–MICHEL SCHÖNBERG
Lyrics by ALAIN BOUBLIL, JEAN-MARC NATEL
and HERBERT KRETZMER

cook-ing the books. _ Sel-dom do you see
light-en your purse. _ Here the goose is cooked.

hon-est men like me, a gent of good in - tent who's con -
Here the fat is fried. And noth-ing's o - ver - looked till I'm

tent to be... Mas - ter of the house,
sat - is - fied... Food be - yond com - pare,

dol - ing out the charm read - y with a hand-shake and an o - pen palm.
food be - yond be - lief, mix it in a min - cer and pre tend it's beef.

Tells a sauc-y tale, makes a lit-tle stir, cus-tom-ers ap-pre-ci-ate a
Kid-ney of a horse, liv-er of a cat, fill-ing up the sau-sa-ges with

B7 **E**

bon vi-veur. Glad to do a friend a fa - vor. Does-n't cost me to be nice.
this and that. Res - i-dents are more than wel - come. Bri-dal suite is oc - cu - pied.

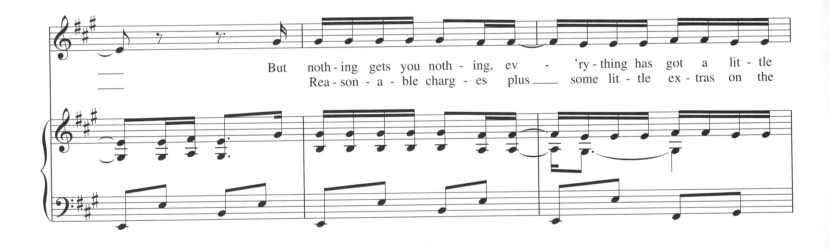

But noth-ing gets you noth-ing, ev - 'ry-thing has got a lit-tle
Rea - son-a - ble charg - es plus some lit-tle ex-tras on the

A

price. Mas - ter of the house, keep-er of the zoo,
side. Charge 'em for the lice, ex - tra for the mice,

ev-'ry-bod-y's chap-er-one. ___ / Give'em ev-'ry-thing I've got. ___

But lock up your va-lis-es. Je - sus, won't I skin you to the / Dir-ty bunch of geez-ers, Je - sus, what a sor-ry lit-tle

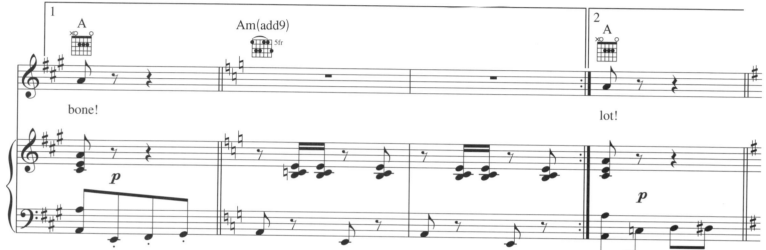

bone!

lot!

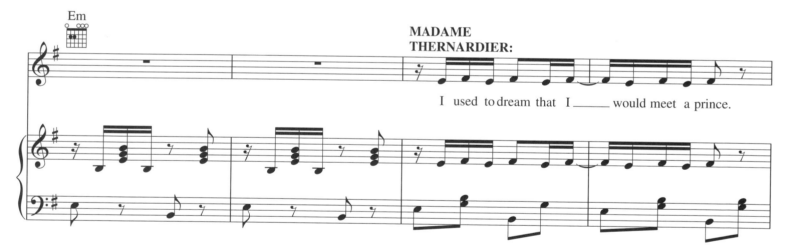

MADAME THERNARDIER:

I used to dream that I ___ would meet a prince.

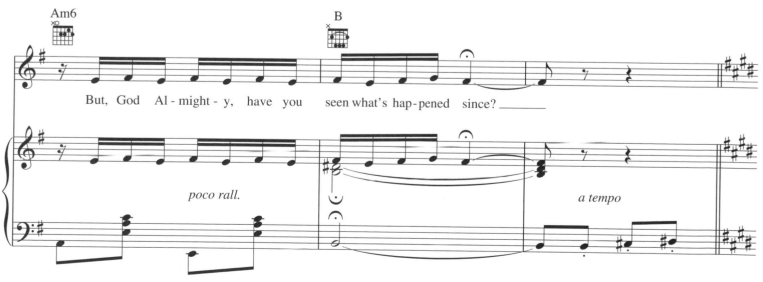

But, God Al-might-y, have you seen what's hap-pened since? ___

poco rall.

a tempo

IN MY LIFE
from LES MISÉRABLES

Music by CLAUDE-MICHEL SCHÖNBERG
Lyrics by ALAIN BOUBLIL, JEAN-MARC NATEL
and HERBERT KRETZMER

Andante

COSETTE:

In my life there are so man-y ques-tions and an-swers that some-how seem wrong. In my

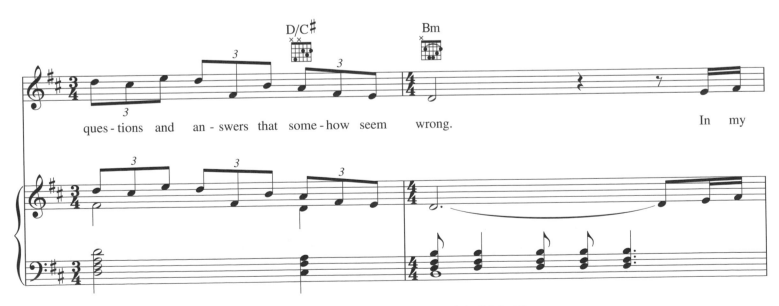

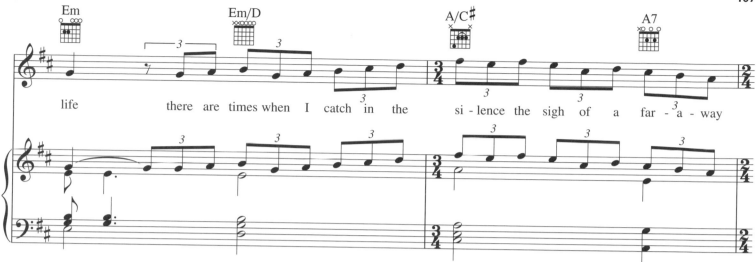

life there are times when I catch in the si-lence the sigh of a far-a-way

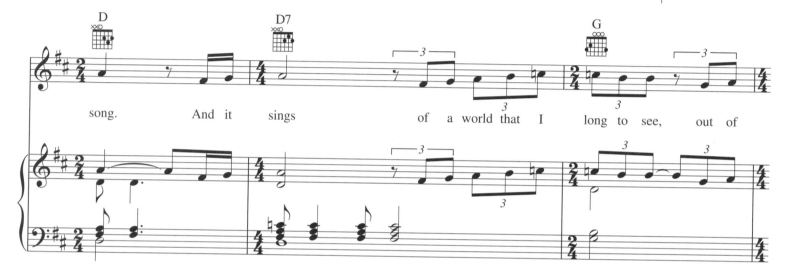

song. And it sings of a world that I long to see, out of

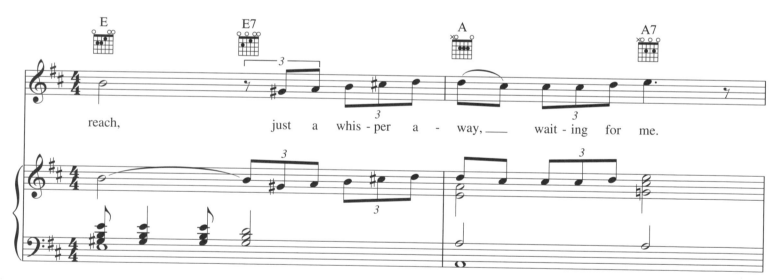

reach, just a whis-per a-way, waiting for me.

Does he know I'm a-live? Do I know if he's real?

Did he see___ what I saw?___ Does he feel___ what I feel? In my

life I'm no long-er a - lone. Now the love of my life is so

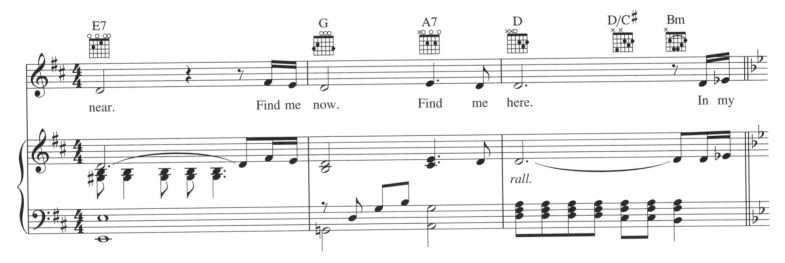

near. Find me now. Find me here. In my

life I have all that I want. You are lov-ing and gen-tle and

good. But pa - pa, dear pa - pa, in your eyes I am

just like a child who is lost in a wood. No more

words. No more words, it's a time that is dead. There are

words that are bet - ter un - heard, __ bet - ter un - said. In my

life   I'm no long-er a   child and I long for the truth that you

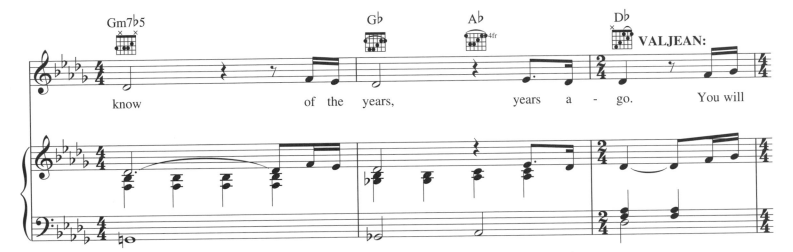

know   of the years,   years a - go. You will

learn.   Truth is giv-en by God to us all in our time, in our

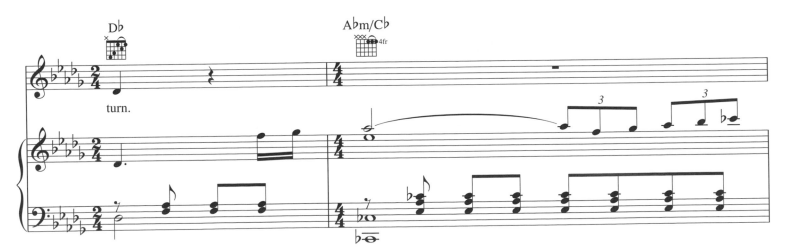

turn.

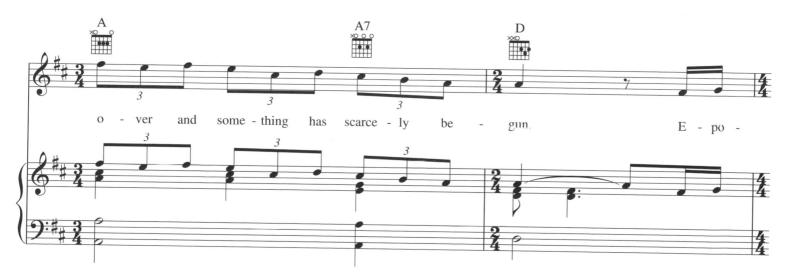

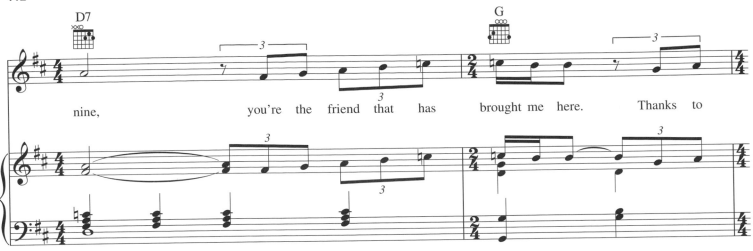

nine, you're the friend that has brought me here. Thanks to

you I am one with the gods and heav-en is near.

And I soar through a world that is new that is free.

EPONINE:

Ev-'ry word that he says is a dag-ger in me. In my

life there's been no one like him an-y-where. An-y-where where he

is, if he asked I'd be

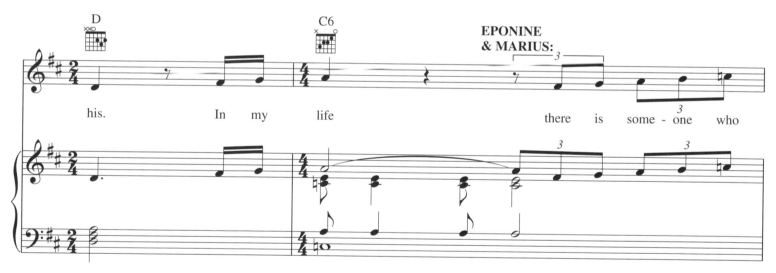

his. In my life there is some-one who

EPONINE & MARIUS:

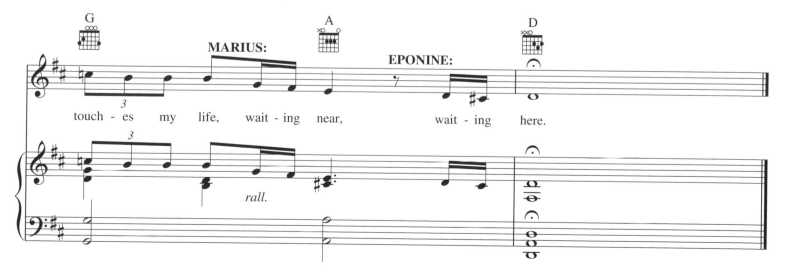

touch-es my life, wait-ing near, wait-ing here.

MARIUS:

EPONINE:

rall.

A HEART FULL OF LOVE

from LES MISÉRABLES

Music by CLAUDE-MICHEL SCHÖNBERG
Lyrics by ALAIN BOUBLIL, JEAN-MARC NATEL
and HERBERT KRETZMER

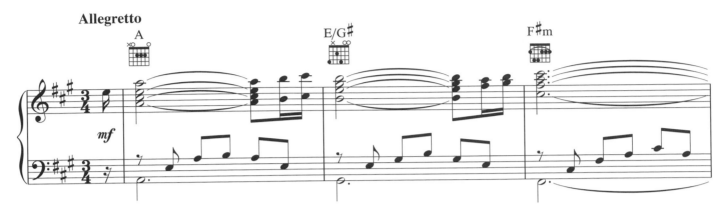

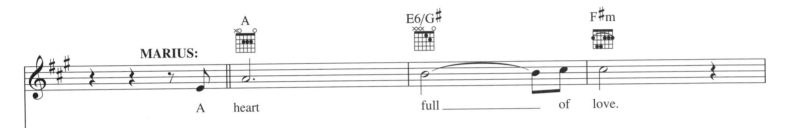

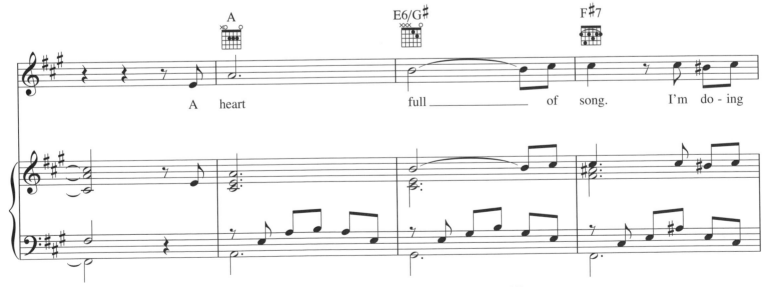

ev-'ry - thing all wrong! Oh God, for shame! I do not

e - ven __ know your name. Dear Mad' - moi - selle,

won't you say? No fear, won't you say?

COSETTE:

A heart

(MARIUS:) Will you

poco rall. *a tempo*

full __ of love. No fear,

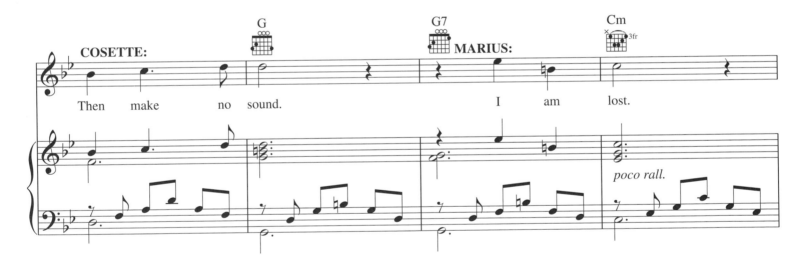

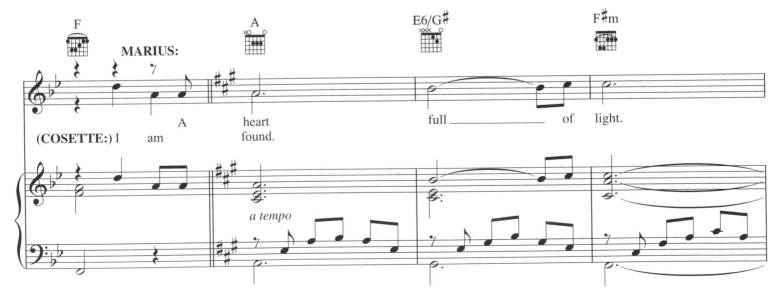

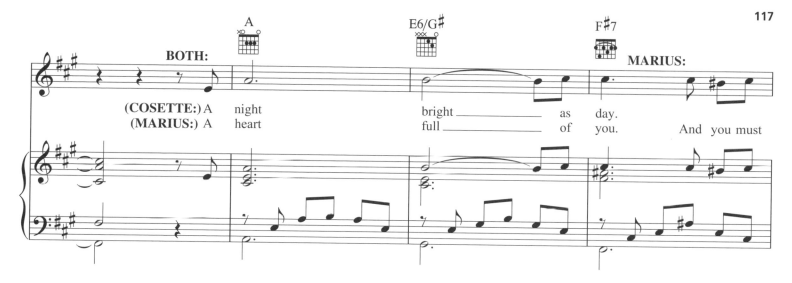

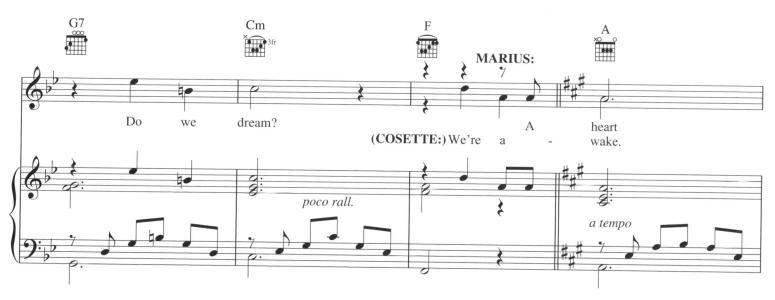

full _____ of love.
(EPONINE:) He was nev-er mine to lose. A heart
MARIUS & COSETTE: A

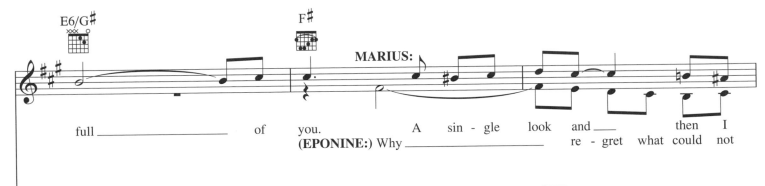

full _____ of you. A sin-gle look and ___ then I
(EPONINE:) Why _____ re-gret what could not
MARIUS:

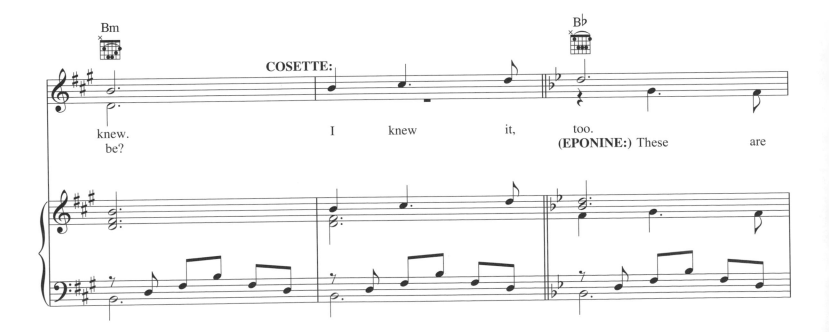

knew. I knew it, too.
be? **COSETTE:** **(EPONINE:)** These are

STARS
from LES MISÉRABLES

Music by CLAUDE-MICHEL SCHÖNBERG
Lyrics by HERBERT KRETZMER and ALAIN BOUBLIL

BRING HIM HOME

from LES MISÉRABLES

Music by CLAUDE-MICHEL SCHÖNBERG
Lyrics by HERBERT KRETZMER and ALAIN BOUBLIL

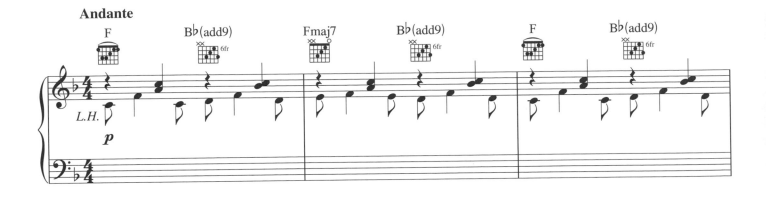

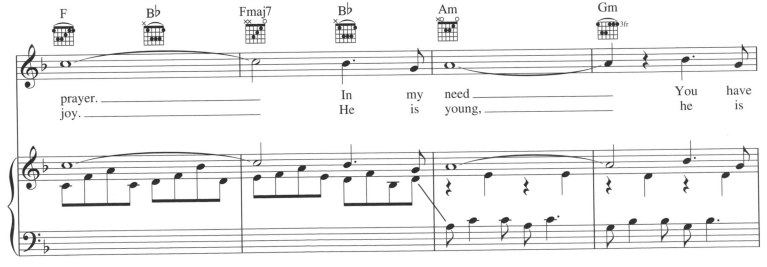

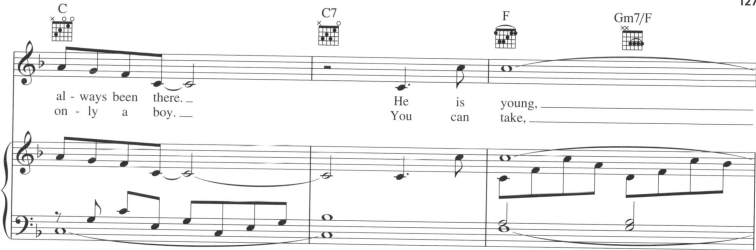

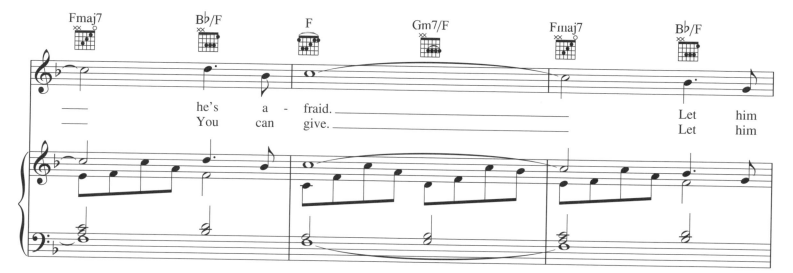

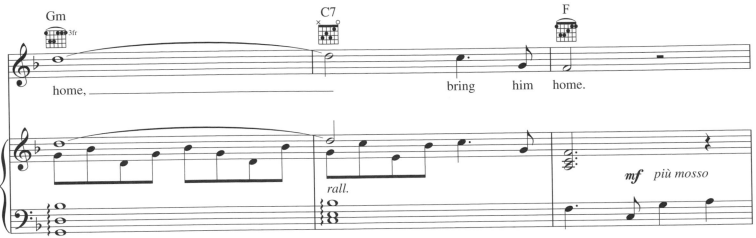

home, _____ bring him home.

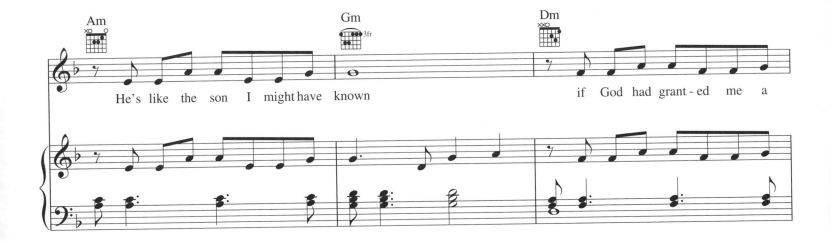

He's like the son I might have known if God had grant-ed me a

son. The sum-mers die one by one. How soon they

fly on and on. And I am old and will be

129

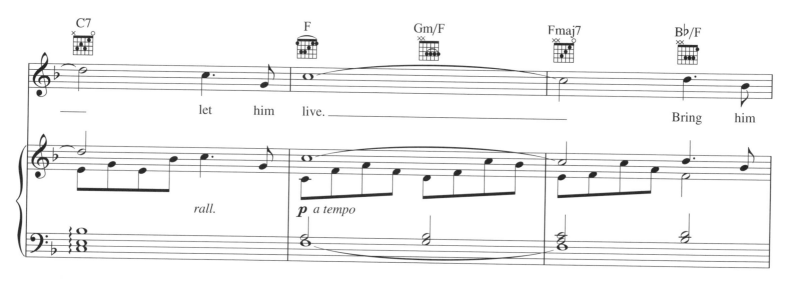

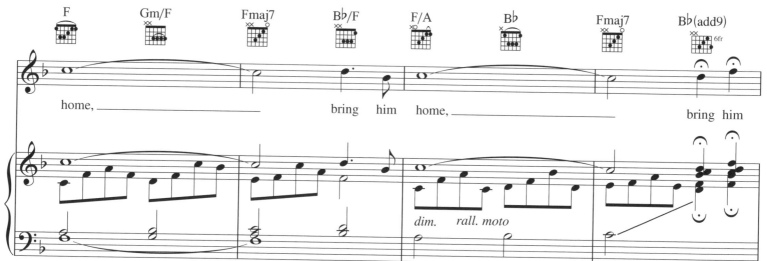

ONE DAY MORE

from LES MISÉRABLES

Music by CLAUDE-MICHEL SCHÖNBERG
Lyrics by ALAIN BOUBLIL, JEAN-MARC NATEL
and HERBERT KRETZMER

day, how can I live when we are part-ed? **VALJEAN:** One day

MARIUS: **COSETTE:** more. To-mor-row you'll be worlds a-way, and yet with you my world has

start-ed. **EPONINE:** One more day all on my own. **M:** **C:** Will we ev-er meet a-

EP: gain? One more day with him not car-ing. **M:** **C:** I was born to be with you. **EP:** What a life I might have

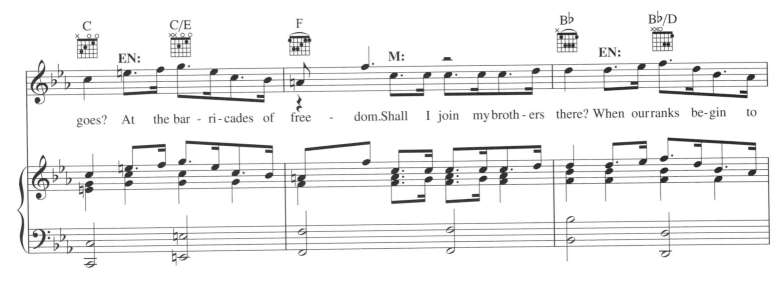

now _____ the day _____ is here! One day

JAVERT:
more. One more day to rev-o-lu-tion, we will nip it in the bud. We'll be read-y for these

(JAV:) school boys, they will wet them-selves with blood.   **THÉNARDIERS:**

JV: One day more.   Watch 'em run a-muck,   catch 'em as they

fall,   nev-er know your luck when there's a free-for-all.   Here a lit-tle "dip,"   there a lit-tle

Bm7   E   F#   F#/A#   **GROUP 1:**

"touch." Most of them are gon-ers so they won't miss much. One day to a new be-

Bm   **GROUP 2:**   F#   **G1:**   F#/A#   B   **G2:**

gin-ning. Raise the flag of free-dom high. Ev-ery man will be a king! Ev-ery man will be a

E   **G1:**   E/G#   Am   **G2:**   Am/C   E   **G1:**   E/G#   **G2:**

king! There's a new world for the win-ning, there's a new world to be won. Do you hear the peo-ple

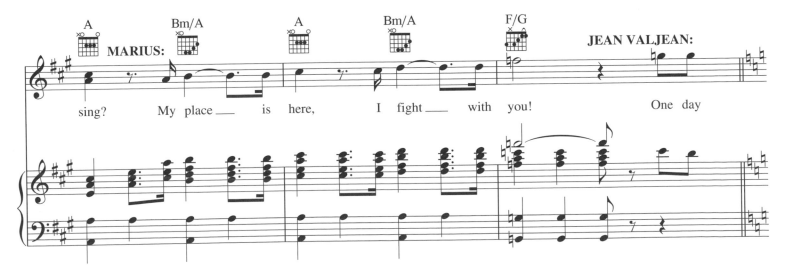

A   **MARIUS:**   Bm/A   A   Bm/A   F/G   **JEAN VALJEAN:**

sing? My place is here, I fight with you! One day

F   F/E   Dm7   Dm/G

EP: own.

M:
C: How can I live ___ when we are part - ed?

JV: One day

JAV: go. I will learn their lit - tle se - crets, I will know the things they

TH's: here a lit - tle "dip," there a lit - tle "touch,"

mor - row we'll dis - cov - er what our God in heav - en has in store. One more

dawn. One more day. One day

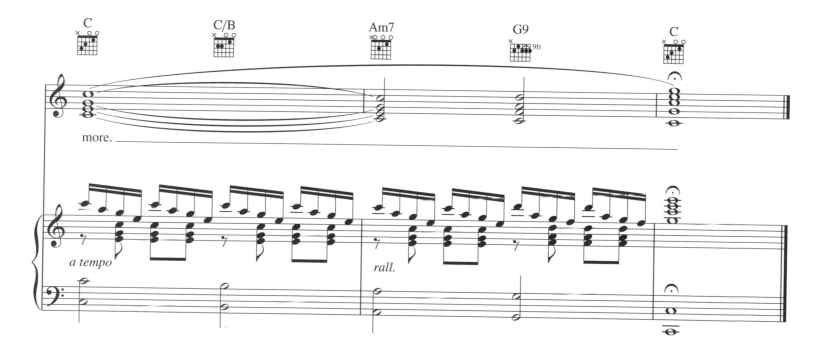

more.

DO YOU HEAR THE PEOPLE SING?

from LES MISÉRABLES

Music by CLAUDE-MICHEL SCHÖNBERG
Lyrics by ALAIN BOUBLIL, JEAN-MARC NATEL
and HERBERT KRETZMER

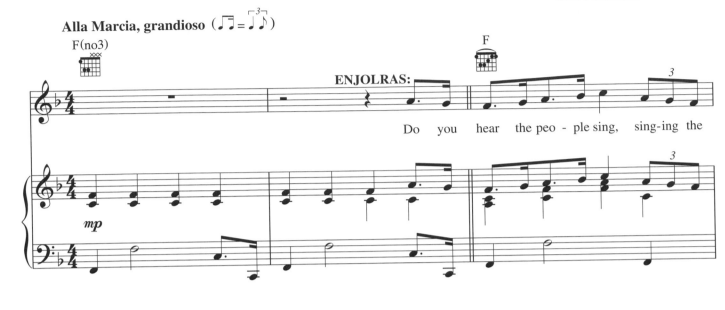

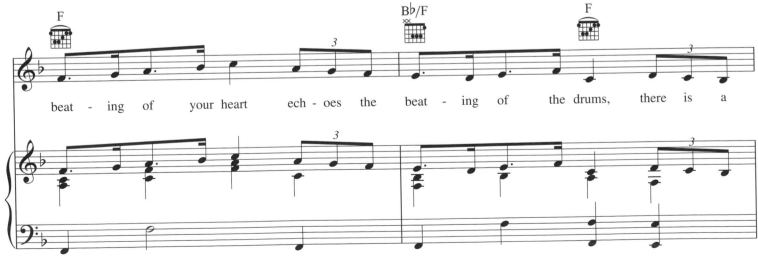

song of an - gry men? It is the mu - sic of a peo - ple who will not be slaves a - gain! When the

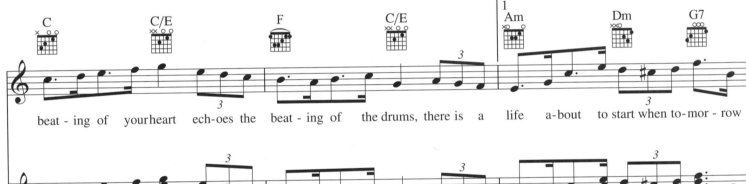

beat - ing of your heart ech-oes the beat - ing of the drums, there is a life a-bout to start when to-mor - row

comes!   FEUILLY: Will you life a-bout to start when to-mor - row comes!